Thomas Bailey Aldrich

Mercedes and later lyrics

Thomas Bailey Aldrich
Mercedes and later lyrics
ISBN/EAN: 9783742897619

Manufactured in Europe, USA, Canada, Australia, Japa

Cover: Foto ©Thomas Meinert / pixelio.de

Manufactured and distributed by brebook publishing software (www.brebook.com)

Thomas Bailey Aldrich

Mercedes and later lyrics

THOMAS BAILEY ALDRICH

MERCEDES, AND LATER LYRICS

BOSTON
HOUGHTON, MIFFLIN AND COMPANY
New York: 11 East Seventeenth Street
The Riverside Press, Cambridge
1884

CONTENTS.

MERCEDES.   PAGE

  I. The Bivouac 11

  II. At Arguano 28

ON LYNN TERRACE, ETC.

  On Lynn Terrace 59

  The Jew's Gift 63

  Pepita 68

  Bayard Taylor 72

INTAGLIOS.

  Intaglios 77

  Epics and Lyrics 79

  Heredity 80

  Myrtilla 82

  On her Blushing 82

  One Woman 83

  Prescience 84

  Epigram 86

CONTENTS.

	PAGE
A Preacher	87
Comedy	89
Kriss Kringle	91
Discipline	92
Appreciation	94
The Voice of the Sea	95
Knowledge	97
In the Belfry of the Nieuwe Kerk	98
Apparitions	100
Realism	101
The Bells at Midnight	102

EPILOGUE.

At Twoscore	107

MERCEDES.

An incident related in the *Mémoirs* of the Duchess d'Abrantès suggested this sketch. The love story which forms the basis of the plot, the characterization of the persons represented in the episode, and its dramatic action are the writer's.

CHARACTERS.

ACHILLE LOUVOIS.

LABOISSIÈRE.

PADRE JOSÉF.

MERCEDES.

URSULA.

SERGEANT & SOLDIERS.

Scene: Spain.   Period: 1810.

MERCEDES.

ACT I.

A detachment of French troops bivouacked on the edge of the forest of Covelleda. — A sentinel is seen on the cliffs overhanging the camp. — The guard is relieved in dumb-show as the dialogue progresses. — Louvois and Laboissière, wrapped in great-coats, are seated by a smouldering fire of brushwood in the foreground. — Starlight.

Scene I.

LOUVOIS, LABOISSIÈRE.

LABOISSIÈRE.

Louvois!

LOUVOIS, starting from a reverie.

Eh? What is it? I must have slept.

LABOISSIÈRE.

With eyes staring at nothing, like an Egyptian idol! This is not amusing. You are as gloomy to-night as an undertaker out of employment.

LOUVOIS.

Say, rather, an executioner who loathes his trade. No, I was not asleep. I cannot sleep with this business on my conscience.

LABOISSIÈRE.

In affairs like this, conscience goes to the rear—with the sick and wounded.

LOUVOIS.

One may be forgiven, or can forgive himself, many a cruel thing done in the heat of battle; but to steal upon a defenseless village, and in cold blood sabre old men, women, and children —that revolts me.

LABOISSIÈRE.

What must be, must be.

LOUVOIS.

Yes—the poor wretches.

LABOISSIÈRE.

The orders are—

LOUVOIS.

Every soul!

LABOISSIÈRE.

They have brought it upon themselves, if that comforts them. Every defile in these infernal mountains bristles with carabines; every village gives shelter or warning to the guerrillas. The army is being decimated by assassination. It is the same ghastly story throughout Castile and Estremadura. After we have taken a town we lose more men than it cost us to storm it. I would rather look into the throat of a battery at forty paces than attempt to pass through certain streets in Madrid or Burgos after night-fall. You go in at one end, but, *diantre!* you don't come out at the other.

LOUVOIS.

What would you have? It is life or death with these people.

LABOISSIÈRE.

I would have them fight like Christians. Poisoning water-courses is not fighting, and assassination is not war. Some such blow as we are about to strike is the sort of rude surgery the case demands.

LOUVOIS.

Certainly the French army on the Peninsula is in a desperate strait. The men are worn out contending against shadows, and disheartened by victories that prove more disastrous than defeats in other lands.

LABOISSIÈRE.

It is the devil's own country. The very birds here have no song.[1] Even the cigars are damnable. Will you have one?

LOUVOIS.

Thanks, no.

LABOISSIÈRE, after a pause.

This village of Arguano which we are to dis-

---

[1] Except in a few provinces, singing-birds are rare in Spain, owing to the absence of woodland.

cipline, as the brave Junot would say, is it much of a village?

LOUVOIS.

No; an insignificant hamlet — one wide *calle* with a zigzag line of stucco houses on each side; a posada, and a forlorn chapel standing like an overgrown tombstone in the middle of the cemetery. In the market-place, three withered olive trees. On a hilltop overlooking all, a windmill of the time of Don Quixote. In brief, the regulation Spanish village.

LABOISSIÈRE.

You have been there, then? — with your three withered olive trees!

LOUVOIS, slowly.

Yes, I have been there. . . .

LABOISSIÈRE, aside.

He has that same odd look in his eyes which has puzzled me these two days. (Aloud.) If I have touched a wrong chord. pardon! You have unpleasant associations with the place.

LOUVOIS.

I? O, no; on the contrary I have none but agreeable memories of Arguano. I was quartered there, or, rather, in the neighborhood, for several weeks a year or two ago. I was recovering from a wound at the time, and the air of that valley did me better service than a platoon of surgeons. Then the villagers were simple, honest folk — for Spaniards. Indeed, they were kindly folk. I remember the old padre, he was not half a bad fellow, though I have no love for the long-gowns. With his scant black soutane, and his thin white hair brushed behind his ears under a skull-cap, he somehow reminded me of my old mother in Languedoc, and we were good comrades. We used now and then to empty a bottle of Valdepeñas together in the shady posada garden. The native wine here, when you get it pure, betters expectation.

LABOISSIÈRE.

Why, that was consorting with the enemy! The Church is our deadliest foe now. Since

the bull of Pius VII., excommunicating the
Emperor, we all are heretical dogs in Spanish
eyes. His Holiness has made murder a short-
cut to heaven.[1] By poniarding or poisoning a
Frenchman, these fanatics fancy that they in-
sure their infinitesimal souls.

LOUVOIS.

Yes, they believe that; yet when all is said,
I have no great thirst for this poor padre's
blood. If the maréchal had only turned over
to me some other village! No — I do not mean
what I say. Since the work was to be done, it
was better I should do it. There's a fatality
in sending me to Arguano. Remember that.
From the moment the order came from head-
quarters I have had such a heaviness here.
(Pauses.) Awhile ago, in a half doze, I dreamed

[1] In Andalusia, and in fact throughout Spain at that period, the priests taught the children a catechism of which this is a specimen: "How many Emperors of the French are there?" "One actually, in three deceiving persons." — "What are they called?" "Napoleon, Murat, and Manuel Godoy, Prince of the Peace." — "Which is the most wicked?" "They are all equally so." — "What are the French?" "Apostate Christians turned heretics." — "What punishment does a Spaniard deserve who fails in his duty?" "The death and infamy of a traitor." — "Is it a sin to kill a Frenchman?" "No, my father; heaven is gained by killing one of these heretical dogs."

of cutting down this harmless old priest who had come to me to beg mercy for the women and children. I cut him across the face, Laboissière! I saw him still smiling, with his lip slashed in two. The irony of it! When I think of that smile I am tempted to break my sword over my knee, and throw myself into the ravine yonder.

LABOISSIÈRE, aside.

This is the man who got the cross for sabring three gunners in the trench at Saragossa! It is droll he should be so moved by the idea of killing a beggarly old Jesuit more or less. (Aloud.) Bah! it was only a dream, *voilà tout* — one of those villainous nightmares which run wild over these hills. I have been kicked by them myself many a time. What, the devil! dreams always go by contraries; in which case you will have the satisfaction of being knocked on the head by the venerable padre — and so quits. It may come to that. Who knows? We are surrounded by spies; I would wager a week's rations that Arguano is prepared for us.

LOUVOIS.

If I thought that! An assault with resistance would cover all. Yes, yes — the spies. They must be aware of our destination and purpose. A movement such as this could not have been made unobserved. (Abruptly.) Laboissière!

Well?

LABOISSIÈRE.

LOUVOIS.

There was a certain girl at Arguano, a niece or god-daughter to the old padre — a brave girl.

LABOISSIÈRE.

Ah — so? Come now, confess, my captain, it was the *sobrina,* and not the old priest, you struck down in your dream.

LOUVOIS.

Yes, that *was* it. How did you know?

LABOISSIÈRE.

By instinct and observation. There is always a woman at the bottom of everything. You have only to go deep enough.

LOUVOIS.

This girl troubles me. I was ordered from Arguano without an instant's warning — at midnight — between two breaths, as it were. Then communication with the place was cut off. . . . I have never heard word of her since.

LABOISSIÈRE.

So? Did you love her?

LOUVOIS.

I have not said that.

LABOISSIÈRE.

Speak your thought, and say it. I ever loved a love-story, when it ran as clear as a trout-brook and had the right heart-leaps in it. With this wind sighing in the tree-tops, and these heavy stars drooping over us, it is the very place and hour for a bit of romance. Come, now.

LOUVOIS.

It was all of a romance.

LABOISSIÈRE.

I knew it! I will begin for you: You loved her.

LOUVOIS.

Yes, I loved her! It was the good God that sent her to my bedside. She nursed me day and night. She brought me back to life. . . . I know not how it happened; the events have no sequence in my memory. I had been wounded; I dropped from the saddle as we entered the village, and was carried for dead into one of the huts. Then the fever took me. . . . Day after day I plunged from one black abyss into another, my wits quite gone. At odd intervals I was conscious of some one bending over me. Now it seemed to be a demon, and now a white-hooded sister of the Sacred Heart at Paris. Oftener it was that madonna above the altar in the old mosque at Cordova. Such strange fancies take men with gunshot wounds! One night I awoke in my senses, and there she sat, with her fathomless eyes fixed upon my face, like a statue of pity. You know those narrow, melting eyes these women have, with a dash of Arab fire in them. . . .

LABOISSIÈRE.

Know them? Sacrebleu!

LOUVOIS.

The first time I walked out she led me by the hand, I was so very weak, like a little child learning to walk. It was spring, the skies were blue, the almonds were in blossom, the air was like wine. Great heaven! how beautiful and fresh the world was, as if God had just made it! From time to time I leaned upon her shoulder, not thinking of her. . . . Later I came to know her — a saint in disguise, a peasant-girl with the instincts of a duchess!

LABOISSIÈRE.

They are always like that, saints and duchesses — by brevet! I fell in with her own sister at Barcelona. Look you — braids of purple-black hair and the complexion of a newly-minted napoleon! I forget her name. (Knitting his brows.) Paquita . . . Mariquita? It was something-quita, but no matter.

LOUVOIS.

How it all comes back to me! The wild footpaths in the haunted forest of Covelleda; the broken Moorish water-tank, in the plaza, against which we leaned to watch the gypsy dances; the worn stone-step of the cottage, where we sat of evenings with guitar and cigarette! What simple things make a man forget that his grave lies in front of him! (Pauses.) There was a lover, a contrabandista, or something — a fellow who might have played the spadassin in one of Lope de Vega's cloak-and-dagger comedies. The gloom of the lad, fingering his stiletto-hilt! Presently she sent him to the right-about, him and his scowls — the poor devil.

LABOISSIÈRE.

Oh, a very bad case!

LOUVOIS.

I would not have any hurt befall that girl, Laboissière!

LABOISSIÈRE.

Surely.

LOUVOIS.

And there's no human way to warn her of her danger!

LABOISSIÈRE.

To warn her would be to warn the village — and defeat our end. However, no French messenger could reach the place alive.

LOUVOIS.

And no other is possible. Now you understand my misery. I am ready to go mad!

LABOISSIÈRE.

You take the thing too seriously. Nothing ever is so bad as it looks, except a Spanish ragoût. After all, it is not likely that a single soul is left in Arguano. The very leaves of this dismal forest are lips that whisper of our movements. The villagers have doubtless made off with that fine store of grain and aguardiente we so sorely stand in need of, and a score or two of the brigands are probably lying in wait for us in some narrow cañon.

LOUVOIS

God will it so!

LABOISSIÈRE.

Louvois, if the girl is at Arguano, not a hair of her head shall be harmed, though I am shot for it when we get back to Burgos!

LOUVOIS.

You are a brave soul, Laboissière! Your words have lifted a weight from my bosom.

LABOISSIÈRE.

Are we not comrades, we who have fought side by side these six months and lain together night after night with this blue arch for our tent-roof? Dismiss your anxiety. What is that Gascogne proverb? — "We suffer most from the ills that never happen." Let us get some rest; we have had a rude day. . . . See, the stars have doubled their pickets out there to the westward.

LOUVOIS.

You are right; we should sleep. We march at daybreak. Good-night.

LABOISSIÈRE.

Good-night, and vive la France!

LOUVOIS.

Vive l'Empéreur!

LABOISSIÈRE walks away humming:

"*Reposez-vous, bons chevaliers!*"

LOUVOIS, looking after him.

There goes a light heart. But mine . . . mine is as heavy as lead.

SCENE II.

LYRICAL INTERLUDE.

SOLDIERS' SONG.

While this is being sung behind the scenes the guard is relieved on the cliffs. Louvois wraps his cloak around him and falls into a troubled sleep.

THE camp is hushed; the fires burn low;
Like ghosts the sentries come and go:
Now seen, now lost, upon the height
A keen drawn sabre glimmers white.

MERCEDES.

Swiftly the midnight steals away —
Reposez-vous, bons chevaliers!

Perchance into your dream shall come
Visions of love or thoughts of home;
The furtive night wind, hurrying by,
Shall kiss away the half-breathed sigh,
And softly whispering, seem to say,
Reposez-vous, bons chevaliers!

Through star-lit dusk and shimmering dew
It is your lady comes to you!
Delphine, Lisette, Annette — who knows
By what sweet wayward name she goes?
Wrapped in white arms till break of day,
Reposez-vous, bons chevaliers!

ACT II.

Morning. — The interior of a stone hut in Arguano. — Through the door opening upon the calle are seen piles of Indian corn, sheaves of wheat, and loaves of bread partly consumed. — Empty wine-skins are scattered here and there among the cinders. — In one corner of the chamber, which is low-studded but spacious, an old woman, propped up with pillows, is sitting on a pallet and crooning to herself. — At the left, a settle stands against the wall. — In the centre of the room a child lies asleep in a cradle. — Mercedes. — Padre Joséf entering abruptly.

Scene I.

MERCEDES, *Padre* JOSÉF, *then* URSULA.

Padre JOSÉF.

Mercedes! daughter! are you mad to linger so?

MERCEDES.

Nay, father, it is you who are mad to come back.

Padre JOSÉF.

We were nearly a mile from the village when I missed you and the child. I had stopped at your cottage, and found no one. I thought you were with those who had started at sunrise.

MERCEDES.

Nay, I brought Chiquita here last night when I heard the French were coming.

Padre JOSÉF.

Quick, Mercedes! there is not an instant to waste.

MERCEDES.

Then hasten, Padre Joséf, while there is yet time.   *(Pushes him towards the door.)*

Padre JOSÉF.

And you, child?

MERCEDES.

I shall stay.

Padre JOSÈF.

Listen to her, Sainted Virgin! she will stay, and the French bloodhounds at our very heels!

MERCEDES, glancing at Ursula.

Could I leave old Ursula, and she not able to lift foot? Think you — my own flesh and blood!

Padre JOSÉF.

Ah, *cielo!* true. They have forgotten her, the cowards! and now it is too late. God willed it — *santificado sea tu nombre!* (Hesitates.) Mercedes, Ursula is old — very old; the better part of her is already dead. See how she laughs and mumbles to herself, and knows naught of what is passing.

MERCEDES.

The poor grandmother! she thinks it is a saint's day. (Seats herself on the settle.)

Padre JOSÉF.

What is life or death to her whose soul is otherwhere? What is a second more or less to the leaf that clings to a shrunken bough? But you, Mercedes, the long summer smiles for such as you. Think of yourself, think of Chiquita. Come with me, child, come!

URSULA.

Ay, ay, go with the good padre, dear. There is dancing on the plaza. The gitanos are there, mayhap. I hear the music. I had ever an ear for tamborines and castanets. When I was a slip of a girl I used to foot it with the best in the cachuca and the bolera. I was a merry jade, Mercedes — a merry jade. Wear your broidered garters, dear.

MERCEDES.

She hears music. (Listens.) No. Her mind wanders strangely to-day, now here, now there. The gray spirits are with her. (To Ursula gently.) No, grandmother, I came to stay with you, I and Chiquita.

Padre JOSÉF.

You are mad, Mercedes. They will murder you all.

MERCEDES.

They will not have the heart to harm Chiquita, nor me, perchance, for her sake.

Padre JOSÉF.

They have no hearts, these Frenchmen. Ah, Mercedes, do you not know better than most that a Frenchman has no heart?

MERCEDES, hastily.

I know nothing. I shall stay. Is life so sweet to me? Go, Padre Joséf. What could save you if they found you here? Not your priest's gown.

Padre JOSÉF.

You will follow, my daughter?

MERCEDES.

No.

Padre JOSÉF.

I beseech you!

MERCEDES.

No.

Padre JOSÉF.

Then you are lost!

MERCEDES.

Nay, padrino, God is everywhere. Have you not yourself said it? Lay your hands for a moment on my head, as you used to do when I was a little child, and go — go!

Padre JOSÉF.

Thou wert ever a willful girl, Mercedes.

MERCEDES.

O, say not so; but quick — your blessing, quick!

Padre JOSÉF.

Á Dios. . . .

He makes the sign of the cross on Mercedes' forehead, and slowly turns away. Mercedes rises, follows him to the door, and looks after him with tears in her eyes. Then she returns to the middle of the room, and sits on a low stool beside the cradle.

Scene II.

MERCEDES, URSULA.

URSULA, after a silence.

Has he gone, the good padre?

MERCEDES.

Yes, dear soul.

URSULA, reflectively.

He was your uncle once.

MERCEDES.

Once? Yes, and always. How you speak!

URSULA.

He is not gay any more, the good padre. He is getting old . . . getting old.

MERCEDES.

To hear her! and she eighty years last San Miguel's day!

URSULA.

What day is it?

MERCEDES, *laying one finger on her lips.*

Hist! Chiquita is waking.

URSULA, *querulously.*

Hist? Nay, I will say my say in spite of all. Hist? God save us! who taught thee to say hist to thy elders? Ay, ay, who taught thee? . . . What day is it?

MERCEDES, *aside.*

How sharp she is awhiles! *(Aloud.)* Pardon, pardon! Here is little Chiquita, with both eyes wide open, to help me beg thy forgiveness. *(Takes up the child.)* See, she has a smile for grandmother . . . Ah, no, little one, I have no milk for thee; the trouble has taken it all. Nay, cry not, dainty, or that will break my heart.

URSULA.

Sing to her, *nieta*. What is it you sing that always hushes her? 'T is gone from me.

MERCEDES.

I know not.

URSULA.

Bethink thee.

MERCEDES.

I cannot. Ah — the rhyme of The Three Little White Teeth?

URSULA, clapping her hands.

Ay, ay, that is it!

MERCEDES rocks the child, and sings:

Who is it opens her blue bright eye,
Bright as the sea and blue as the sky? —
Chiquita!

Who has the smile that comes and goes
Like sunshine over her mouth's red rose? —
    Muchachita!

What is the softest laughter heard,
Gurgle of brook or trill of bird,
    Chiquita?
Nay, 't is thy laughter makes the rill
Hush its voice and the bird be still,
    Muchachita!

Ah, little flower-hand on my breast,
How it soothes me and gives me rest!
    Chiquita!
What is the sweetest sight I know?
Three little white teeth in a row,
Three little white teeth in a row,
    Muchachita!

As Mercedes finishes the song a roll of drums is heard in the calle. At the first tap she starts and listens intently, then assumes a stolid air. The sound approaches the door and suddenly ceases.

Scene III.

LABOISSIÈRE, MERCEDES, *then* SOLDIERS.

LABOISSIÈRE, outside.

A sergeant and two men to follow me! (Mutters.) Curse me if there is so much as a mouse left in the whole village. Not a drop of wine, and the bread burnt to a crisp — the *scélérats!* (Appears at the threshold.) Hulloa! what is this? An old woman and a young one — an Andalusian by the arch of her instep and the length of her eyelashes! (In Spanish.) Girl, what are you doing here?

MERCEDES, in French.

Where should I be, monsieur?

LABOISSIÈRE.

You speak French?

MERCEDES.

Caramba! since you speak Spanish.

LABOISSIÈRE.

It was out of politeness. But talk your own jargon — it is a language that turns to honey on the tongue of a pretty woman. (Aside.) It was my luck to unearth the only woman in the place! The captain's white blackbird has flown, bag and baggage, thank Heaven! Poor Louvois, what a grim face he made over the empty nest! (Aloud.) Your neighbors have gone. Why are you not with them?

MERCEDES, pointing to Ursula.

It is my grandmother, señor; she is paralyzed.

LABOISSIÈRE.

So? You could not carry her off, and you remained?

MERCEDES.

Precisely.

LABOISSIÈRE.

That was like a brave girl. (Touching his cap.) I salute valor whenever I meet it. Why have all the villagers fled?

MERCEDES.

Did they wish to be massacred?

LABOISSIÈRE, shrugging his shoulders.

And you?

MERCEDES.

It would be too much glory for a hundred and eighty French soldiers to kill one poor peasant girl. And then to come so far!

LABOISSIÈRE, aside.

She knows our very numbers, the fox! How she shows her teeth!

MERCEDES.

Besides, señor, one can die but once.

LABOISSIÈRE.

That is often enough. — Why did your people waste the bread and wine?

MERCEDES.

That yours might neither eat the one nor drink the other. We do not store food for our enemies.

LABOISSIÈRE.

They could not take away the provisions, so they destroyed them?

MERCEDES, mockingly.

Nothing escapes you!

LABOISSIÈRE.

Is that your child?

MERCEDES.

Yes, the *hija* is mine.

LABOISSIÈRE.

Where is your husband — with the brigands yonder?

MERCEDES.

My husband?

LABOISSIÈRE.

Your lover, then.

MERCEDES.

I have no lover. My husband is dead.

LABOISSIÈRE.

I think you are lying now. He's a guerrilla.

MERCEDES.

If he were I should not deny it. What Spanish woman would rest her cheek upon the bosom that has not a carabine pressed against it this day? It were better to be a soldier's widow than a coward's wife.

LABOISSIÈRE, aside.

The little demon! But she is ravishing! She would have upset St. Anthony, this one — if he had belonged to the Second Chasseurs! What is to be done? Theoretically, I am to pass my sword through her body; practically, I shall make love to her in ten minutes more, though her readiness to become a widow is not altogether pleasing! (Aloud.) Here, sergeant, go report this matter to the captain. He is in the posada at the farther end of the square.

Exit sergeant. Shouts of exultation and laughter are heard in the calle, and presently three or four soldiers enter bearing several hams and a skin of wine.

1st SOLDIER.

Voilà, lieutenant!

LABOISSIÈRE.

Where did you get that?

2d SOLDIER.

In a cellar hard by, hidden under some rushes.

3d SOLDIER.

There are five more skins of wine like this jolly fellow in his leather jacket. Pray order a division of the booty, my lieutenant, for we are as dry as herrings in a box.

LABOISSIÈRE.

A moment, my braves. (Looks at Mercedes significantly.) Woman, is that wine good?

MERCEDES.

The vintage was poor this year, señor.

LABOISSIÈRE.

I mean — is that wine good for a Frenchman to drink?

MERCEDES.

Why not, señor?

LABOISSIÈRE, sternly.

Yes or no?

MERCEDES.

Yes.

LABOISSIÈRE.

Why was it not served like the rest, then?

MERCEDES.

They hid a few skins, thinking to come back for it when you were gone. An ill thing does not last forever.

LABOISSIÈRE.

Open it, someone, and fetch me a glass. (To Mercedes.) You will drink this.

MERCEDES, coldly.

When I am thirsty I drink.

LABOISSIÈRE.

Pardieu! this time you shall drink because *I* am thirsty.

MERCEDES.

As you will. (Empties the glass.) To the King!

LABOISSIÈRE.

That was an impudent toast. I would have preferred the Emperor or even Godoy; but no matter — each after his kind. To whom will the small-bones drink?

MERCEDES.

The child, señor?

LABOISSIÈRE.

Yes, the child; she is pale and sickly-looking; a draught will do her no harm. All the same she will grow up and make some man wretched.

MERCEDES.

But señor . . .

LABOISSIÈRE.

Do you hear?

MERCEDES.

But Chiquita, señor — she is so little, only thirteen months old, and the wine is strong!

LABOISSIÈRE.

She shall drink.

MERCEDES.

No, no!

LABOISSIÈRE.

I have said it, sacré nom —

MERCEDES.

Give it me, then. (Takes the glass and holds it to the child's lips.)

LABOISSIÈRE, watching her closely.

Woman! your hand trembles.

MERCEDES.

Nay, it is Chiquita swallows so fast. See! she has taken it all. Ah, señor, it is a sad thing to have no milk for the little one. Are you content?

LABOISSIÈRE.

Yes; I now see that the men may quench their thirst without fear. One cannot be too cautious in this hospitable country! Fall to, my children; but first a glass for your lieutenant. (Drinks.)

URSULA.

Ay, ay, the young forget the old . . . forget the old.

LABOISSIÈRE, laughing.

Why, the depraved old sorceress! But she has reason. She should have her share. *Place aux dames!* A cup, somebody, for Madame la Diablesse!

MERCEDES, aside.

José-Maria!

One of the men carries wine to Ursula. Mercedes lays the child in the cradle, and sits on the stool beside it, resting her forehead on her palms. Laboissière stretches himself on the settle. Several soldiers come in, and fill their canteens from the wine-skin. They stand in groups, talking in undertones among themselves.

LABOISSIÈRE suddenly starts to his feet and dashes his glass on the floor.

The child! look at the child! What is the matter with it? It turns livid — it is dying! Comrades, we are poisoned!

MERCEDES rises hastily and throws her mantilla over the cradle.

Yes, you are poisoned! Al fuego — al fuego — todos al fuego![1] You to perdition, we to heaven!

[1] *flames* — to the flames — all of you to the flames!

LABOISSIÈRE.

Quick, some of you, go warn the others! (Unsheathes his sword.) I end where I ought to have begun.

MERCEDES *tearing aside her neckerchief.*

Strike here, señor. . . .

LOUVOIS *enters, and halts between the two with a dazed expression; he glances from Laboissière to the woman, and catches his breath.*

Mercedes!

LABOISSIÈRE.

Louvois, we are dead men! Beware of her, she is a fiend! Kill her without a word! The drink already throttles me — I — I cannot breathe here. (Staggers out, followed wildly by the soldiers.)

SCENE IV.

LOUVOIS, MERCEDES.

LOUVOIS.

What does he say?

MERCEDES.

You heard him.

LOUVOIS.

His words have no sense. (Advancing towards her.)
O, why are you in this place, Mercedes?

MERCEDES, recoiling.

I am here, señor —

LOUVOIS.

You call me señor — you shrink from me —

MERCEDES.

Because we Spaniards do not desert those who depend upon us.

LOUVOIS.

Is that a reproach? Ah, cruel! Have you forgotten —

MERCEDES.

I have forgotten nothing. I have had cause to remember all. I remember, among the rest, that a certain wounded French officer was cared for in this village as if he had been one of our own people — and now he returns to massacre us.

LOUVOIS.

Mercedes!

MERCEDES.

I remember the morning, nearly two years ago, when Padre Joséf brought me your letter. You had stolen away in the night — like a deserter! Ah, that letter — how it pierced my heart, and yet bade me live! Because it was full of those smooth oaths which women love, I carried it in my bosom for a twelvemonth; then for another twelvemonth I carried it because I hoped to give it back to you. (Takes a paper from her bosom.) See, señor, what slight things words are! (Tears the paper into small pieces which she scatters at his feet.)

LOUVOIS.

Ah!

MERCEDES.

Sometimes it comforted me to think that you were dead. You were only false!

LOUVOIS.

It is you who have broken faith. I should be the last of men if I had deserted you. Why, even a dog has gratitude. How could I now look you in the face?

MERCEDES.

'T was an ill day you first did so!

LOUVOIS.

Listen to me!

MERCEDES.

Too many times I have listened. Nay, speak not; I might believe you!

LOUVOIS.

If I do not speak the truth, despise me! Since I left Arguano I have been at Lisbon, Irun, Aranjuez, among the mountains — I know not where, but ever in some spot whence it was impossible to get you tidings. A wall of fire and steel shut me from you. Thrice I have had my letters brought back to me — with the bearers' blood upon them; thrice I have trusted to messengers whose treachery I now discover. For a chance bit of worthless gold they broke the seals, and wrecked our lives! Ah, Mercedes, when my silence troubled you, why did you not read the old letter again? If the words you had of mine lost their value, it was because they were like those jewels in the padre's story, which changed their color when the wearer proved unfaithful.

MERCEDES.

Aquilles!

LOUVOIS.

Though I could not come to you nor send to you, I never dreamed I was forgotten. I used to say to myself: "A week, a month, a year — what does it matter? That brown girl is as true as steel!" I think I bore a charmed life in those days; I grew to believe that neither sword nor bullet could touch me until I held you in my arms again. (The girl stands with her hands crossed upon her bosom and looks at him with a growing light in her eyes.) It was the day before yesterday that our brigade returned to Burgos — at last! at last! O, love, my eyes were hungry for you! Then that dreadful order came. Arguano had been to me what Mecca is to the Mohammedan — a shrine to be reached through toil and thirst and death. O, what a grim freak it was of fate, that I should lead a column against Arguano — my shrine, my Holy Land!

Mercedes moves swiftly across the room, and kneeling on the flag-stones near Louvois's feet begins to pick up the fragments of the letter. He suddenly stoops and takes her by the wrists.

Mercedes!

MERCEDES.

Ah, but I was so unhappy! Was I unhappy? I forget. (Looks up in his face and laughs.) It is so very long ago! An instant of heaven would make one forget a century of hell! When I hear your voice, two years are as yesterday. It was not I, but some poor girl I used to know who was like to die for you. It was not I — I have never been anything but happy. Nay, I needs must weep a little for her, the days were so heavy to that poor girl. And when you go away again, as go you must —

LOUVOIS.

I shall take you with me, Mercedes. Do you understand? You are to go with me to Burgos. (Aside.) What a blank look she wears! She does not seem to understand.

MERCEDES, abstractedly.

With you to Burgos? I was there once, in the great cathedral, and saw the bishops in their golden robes and all the jewelled windows ablaze in the sunset. But with you? Am I dreaming this? The very room has grown unfamiliar to me. The crucifix yonder, at which I have knelt a hundred times, was it always there? My head is full of unwonted visions. I think I hear music and the sounds of castanets, like poor old Ursula. Those cries in the calle —is it a merry-meeting? Ah! what a pain struck my heart then! O God! I had forgotten! (Clutches his arm and pushes him from her.) Have you drunk wine this day?

LOUVOIS.

Why, Mercedes, how strange you are!

MERCEDES.

No, no! have you drunk wine?

LOUVOIS.

Well, yes, a cup without. What then? How white you are!

MERCEDES.

Quick! let me look you in the face. I wish to tell you something. You loved me once . . . it was in May . . . your wound is quite well now? No, no, not that! All things slip from me. Chiquita— Nay, hold me closer, I do not see you. Into the sunlight — into the sunlight!

LOUVOIS.

She is fainting!

MERCEDES.

I am dying — I am poisoned. The wine was drugged for the French. I was desperate. Chiquita — there in the cradle — she is dead —and I —   (Sinks down at his feet.)

LOUVOIS, stooping over her.

Mercedes! Mercedes!

After an interval a measured tramp is heard outside. A sergeant with a file of soldiers in disorder enters the hut.

Scene V.

SERGEANT *and* **SOLDIERS.**

1st SOLDIER.

Behold! he has killed the murderess.

2d SOLDIER.

If she had but twenty lives now!

3d SOLDIER.

That would not bring back the brave Laboissière and the rest.

2d SOLDIER.

Sapristi, no! but it would give us life for life.

4th SOLDIER.

Miséricorde! are twenty —

SERGEANT.

Hold your peace, all of you! (Advances and salutes Louvois, who is half kneeling beside the body of the woman.) My captain! (Aside.) He does not answer me. (Lays his hand hurriedly on Louvois's shoulder, and starts.) Silence, there! and stand uncovered. He is dead!

ON LYNN TERRACE, ETC.

ON LYNN TERRACE,
ETC.

ON LYNN TERRACE.

All day to watch the blue wave curl and break,
   All night to hear it plunging on the shore —
In this sea-dream such draughts of life I take,
     I cannot ask for more.

Behind me lie the idle life and vain,
   The task unfinished, and the weary hours;
That long wave softly bears me back to Spain
     And the Alhambra's towers!

Once more I halt in Andalusian pass,
   To list the mule-bells jingling on the height;
Below, against the dull esparto grass,
     The almonds glimmer white.

ON LYNN TERRACE.

Huge gateways, wrinkled, with rich grays and
    browns,
  Invite my fancy, and I wander through
The gable-shadowed, zigzag streets of towns
    The world's first sailors knew.

Or, if I will, from out this thin sea-haze
  Low-lying cliffs of lovely Calais rise;
Or yonder, with the pomp of olden days,
    Venice salutes my eyes.

Or some gaunt castle lures me up its stair;
  I see, far off, the red-tiled hamlets shine,
And catch, through slits of windows here and
    there,
    Blue glimpses of the Rhine.

Again I pass Norwegian fjord and fell,
  And through bleak wastes to where the sun-
    set's fires
Light up the white-walled Russian citadel,
    The Kremlin's domes and spires!

And now I linger in green English lanes,
   By garden-plots of rose and heliotrope;
And now I face the sudden pelting rains
      On some lone Alpine slope.

Now at Tangier, among the packed bazars,
   I saunter, and the merchants at the doors
Smile, and entice me: here are jewels like stars,
      And curved knives of the Moors;

Cloths of Damascus, strings of amber dates;
   What would Howadji . . . silver, gold, or
      stone?
Prone on the sun-scorched plain outside the
      gates
      The camels make their moan.

All this is mine, as I lie dreaming here,
   High on the windy terrace, day by day;
And mine the children's laughter, sweet and
      clear,
      Ringing across the bay.

For me the clouds; the ships sail by for me;
   For me the petulant sea-gull takes its flight;
And mine the tender moonrise on the sea,
   And hollow caves of night!

THE JEW'S GIFT.

A. D. 1200.

THE Abbot willed it, and it was done.
They hanged him high in an iron cage
For the spiteful wind and the patient sun
To bleach him. Faith, 't was a cruel age!
Just for no crime they hanged him there.
When one is a Jew, why, one remains
A Jew to the end, though he swing in air
From year to year in a suit of chains.

'T was May, and the buds into blossom broke,
And the apple-boughs were pink and white:
What grewsome fruit was that on the oak,
Swaying and swaying day and night!

The miller, urging his piebald mare
Over the cross-road, stopped and leered;
But never an urchin ventured there,
For fear of the dead-man's long white beard.

A long white beard like carded wool,
Reaching down to the very knee —
Of a proper sort with which to pull
A heretic Jew to the gallows-tree!
Piteous women-folk turned away,
Having no heart for such a thing;
But the blackbirds on the alder-spray
For very joy of it seemed to sing.

Whenever a monk went shuffling by
To the convent over against the hill,
He would lift a pitiless pious eye,
And mutter, "The Abbot but did God's will!"
And the Abbot himself slept no whit less,
But rather the more, for this his deed:
And the May moon filled, and the loveliness
Of springtide flooded upland and mead.

Then an odd thing chanced. A certain clown,
On a certain morning breaking stone
By the hill-side, saw, as he glanced down,
That the heretic's long white beard was
    gone —
Shaved as clean and close as you choose,
As close and clean as his polished pate!
Like wildfire spread the marvelous news,
From the ale-house bench to the convent gate.

And the good folk flocked from far and near,
And the monks trooped down the rocky
    height:
'T was a miracle, that was very clear —
The Devil had shaved the Israelite!
Where is the Abbot? Quick, go tell!
Summon him, knave, God's death! straightway!
The Devil hath sent his barber from hell,
Perchance there will be the Devil to pay!

Now a lad that had climbed an alder-tree,
The better to overlook the rest,
Suddenly gave a shout of glee
At finding a wondrous blackbird-nest,

Then suddenly flung it from his hand,
For lo! it was woven of human hair,
Plaited and braided, strand upon strand —
No marvel the heretic's chin was bare!

Silence fell upon priest and clown,
Each stood riveted in his place;
The brat that tugged at his mother's gown
Caught the terror that blanched her face.
Then one, a patriarch, bent and gray,
Wise with the grief of years fourscore,
Picked up his staff, and took his way
By the mountain-path to the Abbot's door —

And bravely told this thing of the nest,
How the birds had never touched cheek or
    eye,
But daintily plucked the fleece from the
    breast
To build a home for their young thereby.
"Surely, if they were not afeard
(God's little choristers, free of guile!)
To serve themselves of the Hebrew's beard,
It was that he was not wholly vile!

" Perhaps they saw with their keener eyes
The grace that we missed, but which God
    sees :
Ah, but He reads all hearts likewise,
The good in those, and the guilt in these.
Precious is mercy, O my lord!"
Humbly the Abbot bowed his head,
And, making a gesture of accord —
" What would you have? The knave is
    dead."

" Certes, the man is dead! No doubt
Deserved to die; as a Jew, he died;
But now he hath served the sentence out
(With a dole or two thrown in beside),
Suffered all that he may of men —
Why not earth him, and no more words?"
The Abbot pondered, and smiled, and then —
" Well, well! since he gave his beard to the
    birds!"

PEPITA.

Scarcely sixteen years old
   Is Pepita! (You understand,
   A breath of this sunny land
Turns green fruit into gold:

A maiden's conscious blood
   In the cheek of girlhood glows;
   A bud slips into a rose
Before it is quite a bud!)

And I in Seville — sedate,
   An American, with an eye
   For that strip of indigo sky
Half-glimpsed through a Moorish gate —

PEPITA.

I see her, sitting up there,
  With tortoise-shell comb and fan;
  Red-lipped, but a trifle wan,
Because of her coal-black hair;

And the hair a trifle dull,
  Because of the eyes beneath,
  And the radiance of her teeth
When her smile is at its full!

Against the balcony rail
  She leans, and looks on the street;
  Her lashes, long and discreet,
Shading her eyes like a veil.

Held by a silver dart,
  The mantilla's delicate lace
  Falls each side of her face
And crosswise over her heart.

This is Pepita — this
  Her hour for taking her ease:
  A lover under the trees
In the *calle* were not amiss!

Well, I must needs pass by,
   With a furtive glance, be it said,
   At the dusk Murillo head
And the Andalusian eye!

In the Plaza I hear the sounds
   Of guitar and castanet;
   Although it is early yet,
The dancers are on their rounds.

Softly the sunlight falls
   On the slim Giralda tower,
   That now peals forth the hour
O'er broken ramparts and walls.

Ah, what glory and gloom
   In this Arab-Spanish town!
   What masonry, golden-brown,
And hung with tendril and bloom!

Place of forgotten kings! —
   With fountains that never play,
   And gardens where day by day
The lonely cicada sings!

Traces are everywhere
   Of the dusky race that came,
   And passed, like a sudden flame,
Leaving their sighs in the air!

Taken with things like these,
   Pepita fades out of my mind:
   Pleasure enough I find
In Moorish column and frieze.

And yet I have my fears,
   If this had been long ago,
   I might . . . well, I do not know . . .
She with her sixteen years!

BAYARD TAYLOR.

In other years — lost youth's enchanted years,
Seen now, and evermore, through blinding
     tears
And empty longing for what may not be —
The Desert gave him back to us; the Sea
Yielded him up; the icy Norland strand
Lured him not long, nor that soft German air
He loved could keep him. Ever his own land
Fettered his heart and brought him back
     again.
What sounds are these of farewell and despair
Blown by the winds across the wintry main!
What unknown way is this that he has gone,
Our Bayard, in such silence and alone?
What new strange quest has tempted him once
     more
To leave us? Vainly, standing by the shore,

We strain our eyes. But patience ! . . . when
 the soft
Spring gales are blowing over Cedarcroft,
Whitening the hawthorn ; when the violets
 bloom
Along the Brandywine, and overhead
The sky is blue as Italy's — he will come !
Ay, he will come ! To us he is not dead.

INTAGLIOS.

INTAGLIOS.

INTAGLIOS.

By the chance turning of a spade
In Roman earth, to view are laid
Bits of carnelian, bronze and gold,
Laboriously carved of old —
Sleek Bacchus with his leaves and grapes;
Bow-bending Centaurs; Gorgon shapes;
Pallas Athene helmeted;
Some grim, forgotten emperor's head. . . .
This one, most precious for its make,
That other, for the metal's sake.

A touch — and lo! are brought to light
Fancies long buried out of sight
In hearts of poets . . . bits of rhyme
Fashioned in some forgotten time

And thrown aside, but, found to-day,
Have each a value in its way . . .
This, for the skill with which 't is wrought,
That, for the pathos of its thought.

EPICS AND LYRICS.

I would be the Lyric
 Ever on the lip,
Rather than the Epic
 Memory lets slip!
I would be the diamond
 At my lady's ear,
Rather than the June-rose
 Worn but once a year!

HEREDITY.

A SOLDIER of the Cromwell stamp,
With sword and psalm-book by his side,
At home alike in church and camp:
Austere he lived, and smileless died.

But she, a creature soft and fine —
From Spain, some say, some say from France:
Within her veins leapt blood like wine —
She led her Roundhead lord a dance!

In Grantham church they lie asleep;
Just where, the verger may not know.
Strange that two hundred years should keep
The old ancestral fires aglow!

In me these two have met again :
To each my nature owes a part:
To one, the cool and reasoning brain ;
To one, the quick, unreasoning heart.

MYRTILLA.

IN THE MANNER OF A. D. 1700.

This is the difference, neither more nor less,
Between Medusa's and Myrtilla's face:
The former slays us with its awfulness,
The latter with its grace.

ON HER BLUSHING.

Now the red wins upon her cheek;
Now white with crimson closes
In desperate struggle — so to speak,
A War of Roses!

ONE WOMAN.

Thou listenest to us with unlistening ear;
Alike to thee our censure and our praise:
Thou hearest voices that we may not hear;
Thou livest only in thy yesterdays!

We see thee move, erect and pale and brave;
Soft words are thine, sweet deeds, and gracious will;
Yet thou art dead as any in the grave —
Only thy presence lingers with us still.

With others, joy and sorrow seem to slip
Like light and shade, and laughter kills regret:
But thou — the fugitive tremor of thy lip
Lays bare thy secret — thou canst not forget!

PRESCIENCE.

The new moon hung in the sky, the sun was
    low in the west,
And my betrothed and I in the church-yard
    paused to rest —
Happy maiden and lover, dreaming the old
    dream over:
The light winds wandered by, and robins
    chirped from the nest.

And lo! in the meadow-sweet was the grave
    of a little child,
With a crumbling stone at the feet and the ivy
    running wild —
Tangled ivy and clover folding it over and
    over:
Close to my sweetheart's feet was the little
    mound up-piled.

Stricken with nameless fears, she shrank and
    clung to me,
And her eyes were filled with tears for a sorrow I did not see:
Lightly the winds were blowing, softly her
    tears were flowing —
Tears for the unknown years and a sorrow that
    was to be!

EPIGRAM.

ON A VOLUME OF ANONYMOUS POEMS ENTITLED A MASQUE OF POETS.

VAIN is the mask. Who cannot at desire
Name every Singer in the hidden choir?
That is a thin disguise which veils with care
The face, but lets the changeless heart lie
    bare.

A PREACHER.

Thus spake the Preacher: "O, my friends,
 beware!
How ever smooth and tempting seems the
 path,
With bowers of cooling shade, the end is
 wrath:
Here 't is unsafe, that 's dangerous footing
 there;
But follow me and have no further care;
Make me your guide, for I am one that hath
Lived long and gathered in life's aftermath —
Experience. I bid you not despair.
Reach me your hands and cast away all doubt;
I 'll lead you safe along the glacier's shelf:
You say 't is dark? 'T is noon-day, I insist;

Besides, I know each pitfall hereabout,
I know each chasm " — just then the Preacher's self
Stumbled and plunged into eternal mist.

COMEDY.

They parted, with clasps of hand,
And kisses, and burning tears.
They met, in a foreign land,
After some twenty years:

Met as acquaintances meet,
Smilingly, tranquil-eyed —
Not even the least little beat
Of the heart, upon either side!

They chatted of this and that,
The nothings that make up life;
She in a Gainsborough hat,
And he in black for his wife.

Ah, what a comedy this!
Neither was hurt, it appears:
Yet once she had leaned to his kiss,
And once he had known her tears!

KRISS KRINGLE.

Just as the moon was fading amid her misty rings,
And every stocking was stuffed with childhood's precious things,
Old Kriss Kringle looked round, and saw on the elm-tree bough,
High-hung, an oriole's nest, lonely and empty now.
"Quite like a stocking," he laughed, "pinned up there on the tree!
I did n't suppose the birds expected a present from me!"
Then old Kriss Kringle, who loves a joke as well as the best,
Dropped a handful of flakes in the oriole's empty nest.

DISCIPLINE.

In the crypt at the foot of the stairs
They lay there, a score of the Dead:
They could hear the priest at his prayers,
And the litany overhead.

They knew when the great crowd stirred
As the Host was lifted on high;
And they smiled in the dark when they heard
Some light-footed nun trip by.

Side by side on their shelves
For years and years they lay;
And those who misbehaved themselves
Had their coffin-plates taken away.

Thus is the legend told
In black-letter monkish rhyme,
Explaining those plaques of gold
That vanished from time to time!

APPRECIATION.

To the sea-shell's spiral round
'T is your heart that brings the sound:
The soft sea-murmurs that you hear
Within, are captured from your ear.

You do poets and their song
A grievous wrong,
If your own soul does not bring
To their high imagining
As much beauty as they sing.

THE VOICE OF THE SEA.

In the hush of the autumn night
I hear the voice of the sea,
In the hush of the autumn night
It seems to say to me —
Mine are the winds above,
Mine are the caves below,
Mine are the dead of yesterday
And the dead of long ago!

And I think of the fleet that sailed
From the lovely Gloucester shore,
I think of the fleet that sailed
And came back nevermore!

My eyes are filled with tears,
And my heart is numb with woe —
It seems as if 't were yesterday,
And it all was long ago!

KNOWLEDGE.

KNOWLEDGE — who hath it? Nay, not thou,
Pale student, pondering thy futile lore!
A little space it shall be thine, as now
'T is his whose funeral passes at thy door:
Last night a clown that scarcely knew to
    spell —
Now he knows all. O wondrous miracle!

IN THE BELFRY OF THE NIEUWE KERK.

(AMSTERDAM.)

Not a breath in the stifled, dingy street!
On the Stadhuis tiles the sun's strong glow
Lies like a kind of golden snow.
In the square one almost sees the heat.
The mottled tulips over there
By the open casement pant for air.
Grave, portly burghers, with their *vrouws*,
Go hat in hand to cool their brows.

But high in the fretted steeple, where
The sudden chimes burst forth and scare
The lazy rooks from the belfry beam,
And the ring-doves as they coo and dream

On flying-buttress or carven rose —
Up here, *mein Gott!* a tempest blows! —
Such a wind as bends the forest tree,
And rocks the great ships out at sea.

Plain simple folk, who come and go
On humble levels of life below,
Little dream of the gales that smite
Mortals dwelling upon the height!

APPARITIONS.

At noon of night, and at the night's pale end,
Such things have chanced to me
As one, by day, would scarcely tell a friend
For fear of mockery.

Shadows, you say, mirages of the brain!
I know not, faith, not I.
Is it more strange the dead should walk again
Than that the quick should die?

REALISM.

Romance, beside his unstrung lute,
    Lies stricken mute.
The old-time fire, the antique grace,
You will not find them anywhere.
To-day we breathe a commonplace,
Polemic, scientific air:
We strip Illusion of her veil;
We vivisect the nightingale
To probe the secret of his note.
The Muse in alien ways remote
    Goes wandering.

THE BELLS AT MIDNIGHT.

SEPTEMBER 19, 1881.

*In their dark House of Cloud
The three weird sisters toil till time be sped.*

I.

CLOTHO.

How long, O sister, how long
Ere the weary task is done?
How long, O sister, how long
Shall the fragile thread be spun?

LACHESIS.

'Tis mercy that stays her hand,
Else she had cut the thread;
She is a woman too,
Like her who kneels by his bed!

THE BELLS AT MIDNIGHT.

ATROPOS.

Patience! the end is come;
He shall no more endure:
See! with a single touch! —
My hand is swift and sure!

II.

FIRST ANGEL.

Listen! what was it fell
An instant since on my ear —
A sound like the throb of a bell
From yonder darkling sphere!

SECOND ANGEL.

The planet where mortals dwell!
I hear it not . . . . nay, I hear! —
A sound of sorrow and dole!

FIRST ANGEL.

Listen! It is the knell

Of a passing soul!—
The midnight lamentation
Of a stricken Nation
For its Chieftain's soul!

EPILOGUE.

EPILOGUE.

AT TWOSCORE.

The leafless branches snap with cold;
The night is still, the winds are laid;
And you are sitting, as of old,
Beside my hearth-stone, heavenly maid!
What would have chanced me all these years,
As boy and man, had you not come
And brought me gifts of smiles and tears
    From your Olympian home?

"The blackest cloud that ever lowers,"
You sang when I was most forlorn,
"If we but watch some patient hours,
Takes silver edges from the morn."
Thanks for the lesson; thanks for all,
Not only for ambrosia brought,

But for those drops which fell like gall
    Into the cup of thought.

Dear Muse, 't is twenty years or more
Since that enchanted, fairy time
When you came tapping at my door,
Your reticule stuffed full of rhyme.
What strange things have befallen, indeed,
Since then! Who has the time to say
What bards have flowered (and gone to
    seed) —
    Immortal for a day!

We 've seen Pretense with cross and crown,
And Folly caught in self-spun toils;
Merit content to pass unknown,
And Honor scorning public spoils —
Seen Bottom wield the critic's pen
While Ariel sang in sun-lit cloud:
Sometimes we wept, and now and then
    We could but laugh aloud.

And once we saw — ah, day of woe! —
The lurid fires of civil war,

AT TWOSCORE.

The blue and gray frocks laid a-row,
And many a name rise like a star
To shine in splendor evermore.
The fiery flood swept hill and plain,
But clear above the battle's roar
  Rang slavery's falling chain.

With pilgrim staff and sandal-shoon,
One time we sought the Old-World shrines :
Saw Venice lying in the moon,
The Jungfrau and the Apennines ;
Beheld the Tiber rolling dark,
Rent temples, fanes, and gods austere ;
In English meadows heard the lark
  That charmed her Shakspeare's ear.

What dreams and visions we have had,
What tempests we have weathered through!
Been rich and poor, and gay and sad,
But never hopeless — thanks to you.
A draught of water from the brook,
Or *alt hochheimer* — it was one ;
Whatever fortune fell we took,
  Children of shade and sun.

Though lacking gold, we never stooped
To pick it up in all our days;
Though lacking praise we sometimes drooped,
We never asked a soul for praise.
The exquisite reward of song
Was song — the self-same thrill and glow
Which to unfolding flowers belong,
    And wrens and thrushes know!

I tried you once — the day I wed:
Dear Muse, do you remember how
You rose in haste, and turned and fled,
With sudden-knitted, scornful brow?
But you relented, smiled, at last
Returned, and, with your tears half dried,
"Ah well, she cannot take the Past,
    Though she have all beside!"

What gilt-winged hopes have taken flight,
And dropped, like Icarus, in mid-sky!
What cloudy days have turned to bright!
What fateful years have glided by!
What lips we loved vain memory seeks!
What hands are cold that once pressed ours!

AT TWOSCORE.

What lashes rest upon the cheeks
    Beneath the snows and flowers!

We would not wish them back again;
The way is rude from here to there:
For us, the short-lived joy and pain.
For them, the endless rest from care,
The crown, the palm, the deathless youth:
We would not wish them back — ah, no!
And as for us, dear Muse, in truth,
    We 've but half way to go.

www.ingramcontent.com/pod-product-compliance
Lightning Source LLC
Chambersburg PA
CBHW031405160426
43196CB00007B/901